The New Idea of a University

*The Objects of the College shall be to provide ... all branches of a
liberal education ....*

University College of Swansea Charter and Statutes as amended June 1993

*[Universities] began, as is well known, with their grand aim directed
on Theology,—their eye turned earnestly on Heaven. And perhaps,
in a sense, it may be still said, the very highest interests of man are
virtually intrusted to them. ... what is the nature of this stupendous
universe, and what are our relations to it, and to all things
knowable by man, or known only to the great Author of man and it.
Theology was once the name for all this; all this is still alive for man,
however dead the name may grow! In fact, the members of the
Church keeping theology in a lively condition—(Laughter)—for the
benefit of the whole population, theology was the great object of the
Universities. I consider it is the same intrinsically now ....*

Thomas Carlyle, *Inaugural Address*, 1866, pp. 11–12

*But the religious virtue of knowledge was become a flunkey to the god
of material success.*

D. H. Lawrence, *The Rainbow*,
ed. Mark Kinkead-Weekes (Penguin edn, 1995, p. 403)

*The land was lurching like a galleon steered by a drunken helmsman
into the Gothic night of materialism and mailed ballyhoo. The
humanities were spat upon; the Arts trampled under foot, the historic
sense spurned and ridiculed—in all these haunts of Instruction—
those whorehouses of the trades and paid sciences. ... The literary and
historic professoriate were all but starved; but they had a specially
endowed Window Dressing Faculty with twenty-four branches all
of whose professors lived on the scale of Hollywood Stars. It was
insupportable.*

Ford Madox Ford, unpublished novel *Professor's Progress*, 1939,
quoted in Arthur Mizener, *The Saddest Story*, 1971, p. 458